HOROLOGY
on the
HALF SHELL

by

PETER BELIN

with Photographs by

Jim Waring

Designed and Printed by
HENNAGE CREATIVE PRINTERS

Published by
HIGHLAND HOUSE PUBLISHERS INC.

Copyright © 1978 by Peter Belin

International Standard Book Number 0–918712–06–8

Library of Congress Catalog Card Number: 78-55929

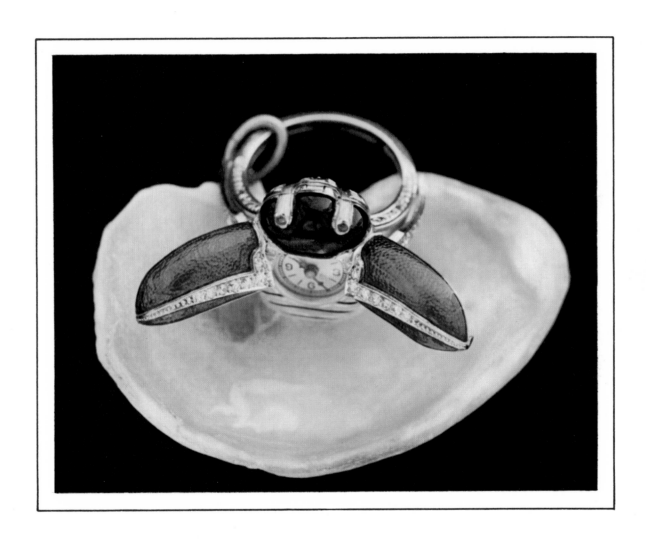

FOREWORD

Please be seated! This pictorial monograph
should be perused in greatest comfort.

ACKNOWLEDGEMENTS

F. LAMMOT BELIN

Creator and preserver of the Arts, he became interested in antique watches in 1917-18 in Peking where he was stationed at the Legation as Secretary to the U.S. Minister, Hon. Paul Reinsch. It was a time when the last dynasty of the Chinese Empire was breaking up and the precious contents of the many palaces were surfacing in the curio shops and bazaars. The facetted smoked-crystal desk watch (Figure 6) is an example of this earliest period of his watch collecting.

During his career in our Foreign Service and during his frequent travels after his retirement, he had many opportunities to acquire all manner of antique watches. But his most outstanding and valuable additions to the collection were made during 1921-23 in Paris when he purchased no less than six examples of the work of Louis-Abraham Breguet—the "Master." From thumb-watch to coin-watch to mandolin-form watch, he sought out every type of portable timepiece and loved them all—frequently permitting his guests to handle these "objets d'art" produced from a specially constructed high-footed drawer-chest in which the collection was "housed." Never did he vaunt these possessions; he loved them and wished to share this love with his friends.

*   *   *

MARY COOTES BELIN

She first became exposed to watch collecting over a 1954 lunch at the Royal Yacht Club in London! Her father-in-law had commissioned her to purchase a small rock-crystal cruciform watch being auctioned at Christie's that day. Her host—Col. Humphrey Quill, Royal Marines, then horologist to Queen Elizabeth II—averred that she might need friendly help "under the hammer"!

Her assistance and encouragement have made this monograph an actuality. Without her warm but ever persistent persuasion, the words, the photographs and the ever-light touch of the subject matter would never have fallen together to make this monograph one small contribution to a fascinating subject.

In addition—and most important—is her incisive concern and knowledge of enamels; of a jeweler's sense of precious metals and stones that fill the eye with satisfaction when wrought into the case of a time-piece; the knowledge and the instinct—when in the "market place"—to pursue or to desist . . . these are attributes that most befit this distaff side of a most exciting adventure, and for which I and the collection shall be forever grateful.

*　　*　　*

JIM WARING

It came to pass that the author was stung by a honey bee—the stinger remaining in the body of the victim! I asked Mr. Waring to extract the weapon and to photograph it; the result—an 8x10 inch photographic enlargement from something much less than the size of a pin-head—convinced me that I had found THE photographer. Mr. Waring was introduced to me by my son who graduated with him from Catholic University in 1973. Subsequently, Mr. Waring worked in an Arlington photographic shop and eventually spent better than three years in the Photographic Department of the National Gallery of Art. His patience with "Stackfreeds" and his artistic competence in reproducing photographically jewels, enamels and even "secret signatures" is proof that the unique character of this monograph lies "with his pictures."

*　　*　　*

PETER A. FRANK

Thanks also to Mr. Peter A. Frank who, under the direction of Mr. Waring, processed most of the color prints from which the color reproductions in this book were made. Mr. Frank's enthusiasm and skill contributed greatly to the accuracy of the color rendition of these watches.

INTRODUCTION

The accurate measurement of time, plus Einstein and others, enabled man to go to the Moon.

This monograph attempts to illustrate earlier efforts of man toward accurate time measurement—specifically the period after "time" became portable and before it became electronic.

1550-1950: 400 years of the mechanical escapement.

TABLE OF CONTENTS

FIGURE 1

First and Last

❀❀

The First

   I Early German Alarm Clock Watch, tambour-shaped (drum) and large, by Sebastian Lehr of Nüremberg.

The Last

  II A 1959 Audemars-Piguet, Grande-Complique with perpetual calendar automatically providing for leap year; minute repeater with full calendar including moon phases and a split center-seconds hand.

*   *   *

The introduction mentions the predominance of the mechanical escapement for 400 years. It may seem ironic, therefore, to start with something of an exception.

Sebastian Lehr is recorded as a town clockmaker active in Nüremberg in 1525; he died in 1556. The watch on the opposite page is an extremely early example of a mechanical "escapement" which word is defined—horologically speaking—as "the mechanism fitted between the main spring and the regulating device of most timepieces." In the days of Sebastian Lehr, when watchmakers were mainly locksmiths, they devised a mechanism to maintain a "regulating device" called the Stackfreed. This looks somewhat like a flattened metal tear-drop which revolves against a straight-line spring that is fixed at one end and that has a roller wheel at the other. (A more detailed description of the Stackfreed appears subsequently, as well as its photographic enlargement on the following page (Figure 2).)

It is clearly evident why this must be a watch. At the "12 o'clock" position there is affixed to the bezel (the outer circular band between the face and back of a watch containing, generally speaking, the works of a watch) a small gilt metal ring through which a chain or necklace was passed so that the mechanism could be suspended from a person's

FIGURE 2

neck. Rumor has it that normally this person was not the owner himself; but rather his servant or pageboy who faithfully followed him carrying this 16th century status symbol so that the proud owner would not be encumbered by its weight or size. However, there is no proof of the foregoing and on the contrary, a knowledgeable horologist states as follows: "Surely the *owner,* not his servant, always carried his watch in the earliest times. I have never seen any painting or engraving of early times to support the idea that the servant carried these precious, decorative and expensive status symbols."

At last, however, "time" had become portable; in the watch there is no pendulum—as there is in most clocks—and although the Lehr does not possess a balance wheel, it does possess its grandfather—the Stackfreed.

The watch industry of the 16th century was centered around the towns of Nüremberg and Augsburg. 16th century watches might have been made in Northern Italy, but there is no known example that can be examined. However, Bassermann-Jordan cites a "Pendant (drum-type) spring-driven *clock, Italian,* possibly as early as 1500" from the Count Lamberti Collection in Rome. Furthermore, many of the early German watches found their way across the Alps to the courts of Italian cities such as Venice and Florence.

In the 16th century, glass was not used for watch crystals; consequently, the Sebastian Lehr has a highly decorated gilt metal cover. It is widely pierced so that the alarm may be clearly heard and it is easy to open in order to read the time by the single hand—in daylight—or by the so-called touchpins at night. In this example, there are two concentric chapter rings (a chapter ring is that portion of the dial on which the numerals appear). Both of Lehr's chapter rings have Roman numerals and, curiously, both use Roman numerals from I to XII. The more normal Stackfreed examples have the inner chapter ring designated from 13 to 24 in Arabic numerals. Apparently, this practice was especially popular in Italy where the philosophers and men of letters were already using a 24-hour designation of time.

This watch is a much traveled one having been in the Henry Levy Collection in 1918, the Percy Webster Collection in the 1950s and the

Charles Kalish Collection in the 1960s. This means that the watch has crossed the Atlantic at least six times. It is reputed to be the earliest *signed* watch in the United States and its movement is entirely made of iron and steel except for two replaced wheels—apparently 17th century repairs. The dumbbell foliot balance * is in "ticking" † condition.

The "Stackfreed"

The Stackfreed is a device for smoothing out the uneven force imparted by a spring as it unwinds.

It must be appreciated that in the 16th century the mainsprings of clocks and watches were very difficult to make. As a result, they were crude and unelastic compared with the products of modern days. A flat spring when wound up in a watch or clock barrel does not give out an even power during the process of unwinding. In the old days a spring which could keep a watch going for some 40 hours exerted too much strength for say 12 hours, then it would give an even pull for about 20 hours, but after that the power would die away to such an extent that the mechanism of a watch stopped. This variation of power caused all early spring-driven clocks and watches to keep very erratic time. They raced away after being wound, then they steadied down and in the final periods the watch lost greatly.

---

* The "dumbbell foliot" looks like a large capital "T" with a small weight at each end of the top bar and is rotated by the force of the spring. In early watches note should be made of the difference between the "cross-bar balance" and the more common dumbbell foliot balance; both of these exist only in 16th century German watches. Gaston Migeon, Curator of Art Objects in the Louvre (1917), in speaking of the "foliot" observes that "it is curious to note that no French document of any kind mentions or describes the foliot."

† Loosely speaking, watches are described in the following stages of condition: (1) running condition—tells time accurately; (2) mint condition—no flaws or missing parts, but a watch which does not necessarily run; (3) ticking condition—where the wheels can be manually energized—generally by pushing on the contrite wheel; and, finally, (4) robbed or suspect—a watch imperfect as to the works, the case, etc.

Clockmakers sought a device to try to even out the erratic pull of a wound spring and thus obtain more uniform time-keeping. The earliest known device was the "fusée," which is illustrated in some of Leonardo daVinci's notebooks of 1480.

The fusée is a conical drum with a spiral groove cut in it.

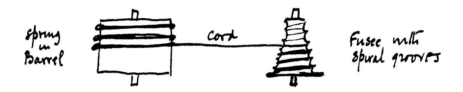

In the diagram the spring is half unwound. When it was fully wound up, the cord would all be on the fusée and the pull of the mainspring would be taken on the *thin* diameter of the fusée, where there would be the minimum leverage. When the spring was nearly unwound, most of the cord would be on the barrel, and that left on the fusée would be wrapped around the large diameter where there would be the greatest leverage. Thus the fusée acts as a sort of gear-box, and arranges that the pull of the spring becomes even.

The early fusées were quite long and thin, and when put in a watch they made the watch very thick and bulky. Hence, watchmakers wanted a device that would even out the pull of the mainspring, and yet would allow the watch to be made as thin as possible. Thus, the "stackfreed" was introduced. It consists of a long steel spring ending in a roller that rolls on the edge of a cam connected by gearing with the arbor or axle of the spring.

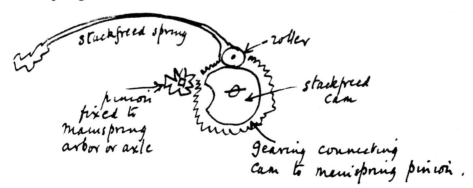

The concept is to shape the cam so that the spring causes *more friction* when the mainspring is fully wound than when it is unwound. Thus, the stackfreed evens out the unequal pull of the mainspring by *varying the friction.*

The early cams (around 1570) were almost circular, but towards 1590, cams became "comma" shaped, which was much more effective,

Stackfreeds are not seen except in German watches, and they died out about 1595, when watchmakers learned to make squat fusées,* as opposed to the old type.† Obviously the gear-box action of the fusée which varied the *leverage,* was much better than the action of the stackfreed which varied the *friction.*

* squat fusees, this

† the old type which were, this.

All stackfreeds are actuated by a verge and crown-wheel escapement in exactly the same way *all* fusées are actuated by an escapement—by the verge, cylinder, duplex, lever, chronometer, etc. A stackfreed and a fusée are only attempts to even out the force of the mainspring as it unwinds; they are a form of gear-box—the mainspring being the engine, but the throttle which controls the engine is, in the case of a timekeeper, the escapement. The escapement, in conjunction with a pendulum in a clock or a balance wheel in a watch, measures out the power dealt by the mainspring in specific and regular amounts each of which is audible as a "tick." A stackfreed, a fusée, or the regulator in the Audemars-Piguet are only refinements to help measure out the "ticks" with evenness and equality during the period between windings of any timekeeper.

The Last (Figure 27, page 56.)

This magnificent and complicated timepiece was purchased by F. Lammot Belin in Geneva from Gübelin in September of 1959. The collection thus acquired a wonderful modern mechanical achievement and a prize piece. Its claim to be a "perpetuelle," however, may be faulted, since the author was emphatically reminded that this "perpetuelle" did not account for the lack of certain Leap Years in the Gregorian calendar. In 1582, Pope Gregory XII struck out 10 days from the then current Julian calendar, and ordained that three Leap Years should be omitted every 400 years. Thus, 1600 A.D. became a Leap Year while 1700, 1800 and 1900 were not; but the year 2000 A.D. will be a Leap Year. Therefore, if this "perpetuelle" be still running, it will remain correct on the 29th of February, 2000 A.D.

However, it is to be noted—most significantly—that time determined by Gregory, still did not coincide with the calendar by a very small fraction. Thus, another Leap Year, in addition, will have to be omitted once in every 4,000 years!

CHAPTER II

Morse Remorse

Innocents Abroad! On 8 February 1963, the antique watch collection belonging to the late Charles H. Morse, Jr. came up for auction at Parke-Bernet Galleries in New York City. This was the first watch auction attended by the author and his wife, and their purchases attest to the meaning of the opening exclamation.

For instance, Lot 110 was described in the catalog as "an engraved brass spherical watch, by Caspar Lindemair, Munich, circa 1680." On best authority, extremely few spherical watches exist today and all were completed not later than 1580. The most celebrated one is currently exhibited in the Musée du Louvre, Paris, dated 1551, by Jacques de la Garde, Loire, France. Almost certainly the example in the Morse Collection is a complete fake and, in addition, altered from time to time as to the works, if not the sphere itself.

Lot 70 was described as "a Louis XVI gold watch with striking automata, Breguet, Paris, circa 1790 . . . inscribed Breguet No. 1359." The number is wrong, and it is doubtful that Abraham-Louis Breguet was manufacturing striking automata in 1790 or, most probably, at any other time.

The Markwick Markham enamel striking watch with Turkish numerals turned out to be far from unique—as the author originally believed—and the dial is very badly cracked which the author did not even observe prior to the purchase! The inner case, however, reveals beautiful Swiss enamelling (Figure 25 page 54).

On the other hand, one of the most astute antique watch dealer/collectors traveled from Switzerland to New York for this sale and acquired an extremely rare and early "Louis XIV emerald matrix and wrought gold watch by Jean Barberet, Paris, circa 1650."

Also in the collection but not acquired by the author was a rare Breguet gold and blue enamel "blind man's. watch" (à tact) set with pearls and rose diamonds. The author has been searching for a similar watch ever since.

Finally, Lot 62, described as a 1735 watch by John Gerrand, London, was contained in an exquisitely enameled case by Huaud le Puisné. This particular watch "resurfaced" at a Zürich auction nine years later, and the 1972 price revealed a 700 percent appreciation in value.

FIGURE 3

CHAPTER III

Harvest and Moses

Illustrated on the opposite and following pages is an early 17th century skull watch—known as a "memento mori." The popular story surrounding the origin of this watch has it that Mary Queen of Scots presented it to one of her maids-of-honor, Mary Seaton—when the latter accompanied the Queen to the scaffold. This fable, while intriguing, is clearly inaccurate; the Scottish Queen, poor lady, was executed in 1587 and one has only to observe the shape of the squat fusée to realize that the works could not have been executed earlier than 1600.

* * *

The auction of clocks and watches—property of the late Percy S. Webster, Esq.—was one of the more fabulous of all time. This auction took place at Sotheby & Co., New Bond Street, London, in 1954 in two sessions—the first on 27 May and the final one on 19 October.

The large silver gilt skull watch illustrated here was purchased on the 19th of October by the London horologist-dealer, Malcolm Gardner, and shortly thereafter became a part of this collection. A good friend of the new owner, F. Lammot Belin, writes a week later, "I have started already to investigate your skull watch and have asked the Museum of Antiquities at Edinborough to put me in touch with the owner of the *other* Mary Queen of Scots skull watch which, however, has not got the crucifix, the arms of France and Scotland, nor the 'SCOTORUM' inscription."

(Hence, the heading of this chapter: (A) the illustrated watch is inscribed "Jehan Moisant à Bloys—an English corruption of Moisant equates to "Harvest"; (B) the *other* skull watch is described in *Les*

FIGURE 4

Horlogers Blésois as being made by Moyse of Blois—thus "Moses.")

Concerning "Harvest," the new owner's friend wrote to Mr. Clarke (who was the auctioneer at Sotheby) for information and he replied that "the fish-skin case, at least, was 16th century in date."

Later that year the owner's friend writes, "I have been in touch with the owner (of Moses) who is a baronet named Sir John Dick-Lauder and who lives in the north of Scotland. He was considerably disturbed that another Mary Queen of Scots skull exists! He says that his family have always understood that the Dauphin of France gave the skull to Mary when they were married in 1558."

In July of 1957, Dr. Derik J. Price—a British expert on horology—visited America and examined this skull watch (Harvest) and he appears to corroborate other experts' opinion that the *other* skull (Moses) is of a later date, circa 1780.

Finally, the new owner's friend writes in January 1960, "I have spent months and months trying to trace that Mary Queen of Scots skull watch (Moses) and only ran it to earth a few weeks ago. It was bought by a rich man who runs a string of fairly cheap jeweler shops throughout England—James Walker. James Walker is in reality a man named G. S. Saunders. I went to see him, but quickly realized that he had bought the skull for himself and for its historical value, and not in any way as something to sell." The friend informed Saunders that he knew a bidder

FIGURE 5

14

willing to offer $10,000 for the skull watch (Moses), but the suggestion was turned down flatly. Finally, "I thought it a pity that this lovely watch (Moses) should be hidden away and so I suggested to the Master of the Worshipful Company of Clockmakers that he should write to Saunders and ask him whether he would consider exhibiting his watch in our museum at the Guild Hall. I am glad to say that he agreed. Last week, I was at Windsor Castle and was talking to the librarian there, and asked him if he would try to get his staff to try to find out what lists of jewels, etc. they have of items which were dispersed when poor Mary Queen of Scots had her head chopped off. The librarian said he would, but added that he was sure in his own mind that he would have heard of it if Mary Queen of Scots had had anything as startling as that large skull."

There is little doubt that confusion still exists as to the authenticity—particularly the date—of this "memento mori" skull clock watch; also the number of similar clock watches that may be in existence—certainly, two are known to be.

FIGURE 6

CHAPTER IV

Horological Platypus

It has been mentioned that one difference between a watch and a clock lies in the fact that the latter has a pendulum whereas a watch does not.

Like the platypus in the animal world, the watch world also has a freak—it is commonly known as the Nüremberg Egg.

This smoked rock crystal pendulum watch came to be known as the Nüremberg Egg through corruption of German into English. Since this watch is German (maker: Jerg Ernst) it was known in German as "Uhrlein"—meaning "little clock"—which is quite logical considering its early date (around 1610 perhaps) and comparing it with earlier "time measurements" known in the German language by the one word "Uhr"—actually for both clocks and watches. Later, when the industry, in part, moved across the English Channel, some imprecise translator described this rock crystal pendant watch as an "Eierlein" which, not unnaturally, became known as "Egg" for "Eier" and Nüremberg as the place of origin—hence Nüremberg Egg.

This watch appears to have a swinging pendulum (Figure 6) which, in fact, is merely a decorated visual automaton—a trinket having nothing to do with the hairspring escapement.

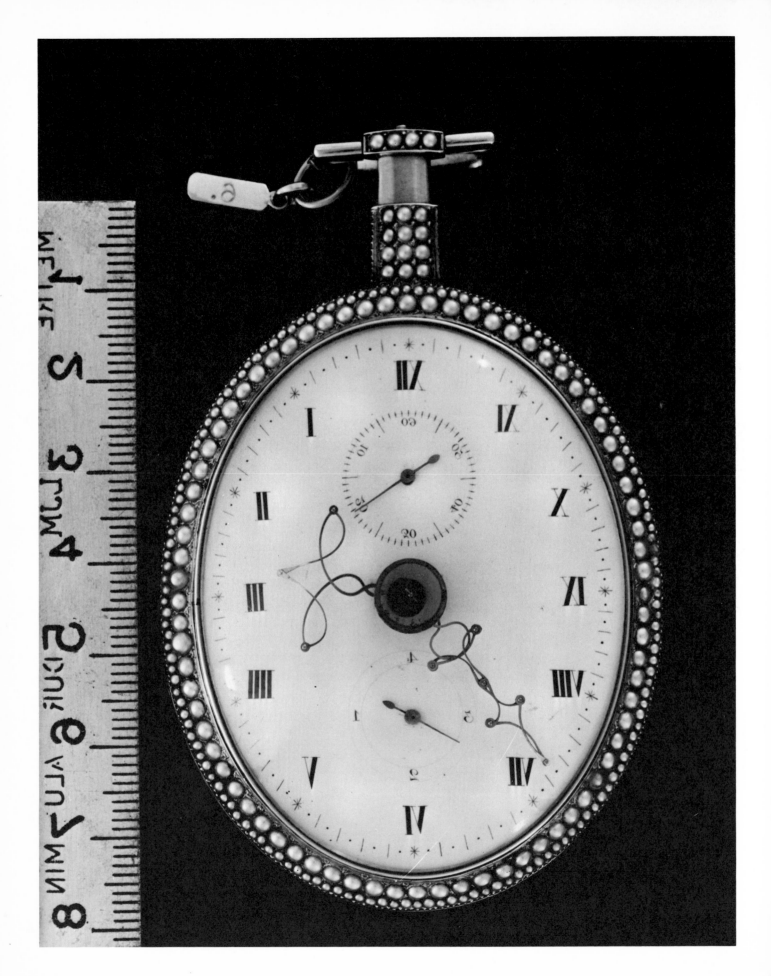

FIGURE 7

CHAPTER V

Watches go to The Beautician

As *Hustler* and other pornographic publications promiscuously proclaim, there follows an eight-page color "center-fold"—bigger than lifesize!

During the 17th and early 18th centuries watches went through many stages of development—not so much scientific theory of the works, but more significantly through size and especially decoration. The inaccuracy of portable time did not change much between 1600 and 1750; on the other hand, the first half of the 17th century saw heavy German steel and silver gilt give way to light and very small French enamel decoration. Watch weight was reduced from some three pounds to something under a quarter of a pound. Enamel of all color and intricacy came in favor as did cut rock crystal cases and champlevé and cloisonné method of decoration.

For example, the Pierre Duhamel, circa 1640 (Figure 8), a watchmaker of Blois, is noteworthy for its unusual rock crystal case, the frame of which is decorated in enamel and the case is lobed and in the form of a stylized chrysanthemum.

The Charles Bobinet (Figure 9), circa 1650, is remarkable for its one inch diameter and for its "mint" condition. It is protected by a most interesting outer case of shagreen—the rounded gold pins of the outer case and piqué showing very little wear, although over 300 years old. The enamel is "en-plein," indicating that the inner side of the watch case is likewise beautifully enamelled. The enamel of the watch-back is attributed to Pierre Huaud père, the father of the more famous Huaud sons—enamellers of the Loire and Paris regions.

This middle 17th century French watch (Figure 10) was made for the Turkish market and therefore, the chapter ring is composed of Arabic numerals. The outer case constitutes a colorful example of cloisonné enamel work—this consists in building up (by thin strips of metal fixed to the ground plate) compartments which are then filled with enamel, thus forming the design. The watch possesses an interesting urn-shaped pendant.

A brown agate case covering a William Ilbery watch of around 1775 appears in Figure 11. The agates are gold framed and there is a decorative center circle of seed pearls. The bow and pendant are of remarkably fine enamel work, as is the bottom stem.

The oval William Anthony is twice illustrated in the monograph, first in color (Figure 12)—the back of the watch—and secondly (Figure 7), a black-and-white rendition of the dial of the watch. This gold-cased watch is outstanding for its blue enamel decoration with seed pearl ovals and a centerstone of topaz. Here again the bow, pendant and accompanying key are of a delicate design and "en-suite"—indicating that all of the watch accouterments are decorated in a similar manner. Turning to the black-and-white picture of the dial of the watch, it should be noted that the hands are jointed and automatically extend and contract as they travel the long and short axes of the oval dial. This remarkable timepiece possesses, in addition, two subsidiary "seconds" dials of different design and movement located along the long axis of the watch.

The Jeffreys and Jones gold and blue enamel watch-châtelaine, circa 1795, set with diamonds and half pearls (Figure 13) is an excellent "modernization" of what some 17th century matrons wore in their belts to which they affixed "the keys of the cupboards." It was in George III's time that men took over this fashion exchanging the ponderous lockkeys for the decorative and symbolic attachments at the extremities of the tassels to include a watch key and family seal, etc., "en-suite."

The last two watches in this chapter (Figure 14 and 15) are the works of Henri Louis Jaquet-Droz. They are both of the latter half of the 18th century and are remarkable for their variety of enamel work—the example (Figure 14) is particularly noteworthy for its paillone or peacock-tail design. The watch (Figure 15) is self-winding which means, in theory, that as the wearer walks, a large metal weight in the interior of the case oscillates to wind the mainspring. Jaquet-Droz was a famous Swiss watchmaker, 1752-1792, from Neuchâtel who worked for a long period of time in London; his famous playing clavicord and portrait-painting automatons still operate in the watch museum in Neuchâtel.

FIGURE 8

FIGURE 9

FIGURE 10

FIGURE 11

FIGURE 12

FIGURE 13

FIGURE 14

FIGURE 15

BREGUET ET FILS

FIGURE 16

CHAPTER VI

April in Paris, 1795

❀❀

There can be little doubt concerning the horological genius of Abraham-Louis Breguet (1747-1823). Some have even referred to him in a quotation: "What Shakespeare is to English literature, Breguet is to watchmaking." Alfred Chapuis—the well-known Swiss author on horology—refers to the "Master": "Breguet was to the watch what Thomas Tompion—two generations earlier—was to the clock."

It is curious that the creative genius of this man bore tremendous fruit during the years 1793-1795 while he was virtually in exile at a small Swiss town near Neuchâtel called Le Locle. To mention a few of his "refinements" that came out of the cold and damp Jurassic hills west of the Lake of Neuchâtel, Breguet perfected the blind man's watch, the ruby cylinder and tourbillon escapements, "perpetuel" or self-winding watches, the automatic quarter repeater watch and, the crown jewel, the "sympatique" clock-watch . . . all this at Le Locle in little better than two years time.

Breguet became an exile from Paris during the Reign of Terror—he was, in fact, a Girondin—something of a Kerensky to Lenin. Thus, when Robespierre and the Jacobins established the guillotine, Breguet's neck was not far from the blade. Actually, Jean-Paul Marat signed a passport for Breguet less than a month before the former was murdered in his bathtub by Charlotte Corday. Breguet's escape stage-coach route from Paris to Geneva was virtually the same route that one follows today—Fontainebleau, Dôle, Les Rousses, Geneva.

At Le Locle, Breguet became acquainted with a so-called M. Monier who had lived for sometime in Petersburg—thus opening the Romanoff market to the House of Breguet. Concurrently his British friends wished him to leave Switzerland for London. But it seems fairly

FIGURE 17

evident that Breguet never abandoned the idea of returning to Paris and giving France the nationality of his watches. To protect them from forgery he obtained the help of his friend, Jean-Pierre Droz—the principal coin designer for Napoleon I, as well as being, slightly earlier, the engraver for the Reign of Terror and its famous "Assignats." Droz invented a pantograph by which Breguet was able to sign his watches in what is generally referred to as "Breguet's secret signature"—see photograph opposite which has the secret signature in Arabic, as well!

Breguet returned to Paris on 20 April 1795 to take over, once again, the direction of his workshop. He appointed his son, Antoine-Louis Breguet, a partner in 1807, but he remained the guiding intellect until his death in 1823.

There are four examples of "Breguet work" in the monograph—the first, "My Lady's Chamber" the pricking ring-watch (Figure 18); the second, by the "Master" (Figure 29); the third by his son, Antoine (Figures 16, 17 and 30); finally, the Breguet marine chornometer (Figure 21—upper half).

Breguet No. 452 is a fine example of a precision timepiece made prior to 1830 (Figure 29). The two-tone, engine-turned silver dial has a "busy" although well-balanced appearance. The fine gold hands and gold moon dial contrast effectively with the silver dial. The moon is recorded as 30 days per month instead of the 29½ usually found on moon registers. The whole is mounted in a fine engine-turned gold case complete with a somewhat rare and finely made winding key—double male (Figure 29).

Breguet No. 3008 (Figures 16 and 17) is a fine gold and enamel pair-case watch for the Turkish Market with "secret signature" repeated in Arabic (both below 12 o'clock). The dial is white enamel with the Turkish numerals in the chapter ring. The watch was couriered to the Breguet representative in 1830 at the Sublime Port, Constantinople, with a second dial—silver, engine-turned and with Roman numerals in the chapter ring. It seems that this "dual dial" procedure was somewhat common practice in order to "hedge" should the Sultanate not be impressed with the timepiece. The back is beautifully decorated with a spiral design springing from a rosette—the spirals being alternating red and white. The back of the outer case of the watch is covered with red, translucent enamel over engine-turning and overlaid with white spokes containing gold laurel leaves springing from a pale blue rosette (Figure 30).

FIGURE 18

CHAPTER VII

My Lady's Chamber

This ring-watch by Breguet is dated 1831 and came to the Collection as a 75th birthday present to the then owner.

Negotiation for the purchase took place in Paris in 1955-56 at the then "Headquarters"—28 Place Vendôme—of the Breguet firm which was, at the time, directed by Mr. Georges Brown who married one of the last descendants of the "Master."

The horological significance of the watch is the fact that it is "keyless"—in other words, a "stem-winder." According to an expert, "It must be a very, very early example of a keyless watch because they did not really start to appear until the middle of the 19th century, and then only in pocket watches."

Then "en-poste" in Paris, Russian Prince Demidoff—the original owner, and presumably inspirator of the watch—was a well-known patron of Breguet's finest horological specimens. And that he gave the ring to his "Princess" opens delightful avenues of speculation!

The "point" being that this *alarm* watch does not sound—it pricks!

When set—and the moment arrives—the alarm releases a needle through a minute hole on the inside of the ring band (Figure 18 opposite). The sleeping—or otherwise—wearer of the ring is thus alerted to the hour with the added advantage of being the sole possessor of this knowledge.

It was the custom in the days of the Restoration for good Paris-folk—noble or otherwise—to have an early morning "café et croissant." Perhaps the faithful "Princess" was performing her matutinal connubial devotion—without disturbing the Prince.

On the other hand, let us suppose the "princess" were not his wife!!

CHAPTER VIII

My Lady's Bracelet

"The wrist-watch has conquered the world!"—or so write Eugène Jaquet and Alfred Chapuis in their book, *The Swiss Watch,* 1945. These eminent author/horologists continue by asking, "What is it's (the wrist-watch) origin?" To answer their own question, they cite an old etching depicting the following story:

"There was a buxom lady installed on a garden bench who was generously dispensing milk to her baby. In order to regulate time of feeding, she attached her watch to her arm. At this point, an observant passerby was struck by such naive ingenuity; he returned home; soldered two brackets to a lady's watch and added a strap!"

In the same book at Plate 88—following page 112, there appears a black-and-white photograph of "the wrist-watch of Empress Josephine embellished with pearls and emeralds and dated 1806."

There appears (Figure 31) a colored photograph of this wrist-watch together with its accompanying calendar to complement the second wrist. This calendar is set daily by a lever at the lower end of the calendar case. The watch is certainly one of the earliest to be designed specifically for wearing on the wrist and it has an early history connected with Josephine who made a gift of this pair to her daughter-in-law, Princess Auguste-Amélie of Leuchtenberg in 1809.

The pair is complete with a small gold and pearl-mounted key by which to wind the watch.

CHAPTER IX

Metric System

With every Department of Highways throughout the United States transforming miles into kilometers, and many industrialists changing inches into centimeters, it is noteworthy that in the early 19th century the French Emperor, Napoleon I, began the fad in Europe.

Bonaparte tried to do it with *time* also—he was exceedingly unsuccessful.

This watch (Figure 26) is an example of the so-called decimal dial which was manufactured during the period of the Directoire. The decimal and calendar dials at 12 o'clock and 6 o'clock, respectively, appear on a decorated enamel face. This face bears the emblems of the French Revolution including the "Cap of Liberty," the "Tricolor," and a column bearing an open book inscribed "la Loi."

During the French Revolution, decimal time was divided daily into 100 "cés"; the "cé" equalled 14 minutes 24 seconds—thus, the decimal dial has a chapter ring of 10 digits as opposed to the conventional chapter ring of 12 digits—also portrayed on this watch dial at six o'clock. The monthly calendar decimal dial has a chapter ring indicating 30 days to every month with no provision for months of 31 days nor for February.

CHAPTER X

Alma Matters

And so does Inkerman!

Napoleon III is not known for his military prowess and, in fact, it is difficult—even for a French historian—to cite French military victories under his reign. The Crimean War of 1853-56 is, perhaps, the one exception, but even here the French were allied with the British and the Turks against the military might of Nicholas I and Alexander II of Russia.

The photograph (Figure 28) depicts the cock of a gold-cased watch by E. Buffat which was created for the Universal Exposition held in Paris in 1867. It is unusual in that the cock is in the form of an "N" and the battles of Alma and Inkerman are commemorated thereon. Visible in the photograph—although not "in motion"—is the revolving "table" of the rare tourbillon movement with its duplex escapement. And not visible in the photograph is the white enamel dial of the face of the watch with its chapter ring inscribed: N.A.P.O.L.E.O.N. I.I.I. The markers of the seconds chapter ring spell the word "Glorie."

Perhaps the most notable monument to have been erected to the victory of Alma is the bridge which crosses the Seine in the middle of Paris. Upstream, on one of the arch pillars stands the famous Zouave in military uniform with musket—possibly one of the first Enfield rifles which saw their initiation on the battlefield in the Crimea. It is a well-known observation that when the Zouave's booted toe becomes invisible due to the rise of the waters of the Seine, most Parisian cellars are flooded.

CHAPTER XI

Key to the Stem-Winder

One of the major modifications in watch making occurred around the middle of the 19th century when watch keys for winding the "running-train" were abandoned and the more practical "stem-winder" came into vogue.

Thus, by means of one piece of mechanism, the owner of a watch could both set and wind his timepiece. Also, it was far more easy to misplace one's key * than to lose one's stem.

Keyless watches, therefore, began to appear on the market just before the War Between the States, and by its conclusion in 1865 every trainman—especially in America—brandished a stem-winder. This American expression—"some stem-winder!"—has remained in the language to denote other "firsts" or "improvements," such as the latest model automobile, hi-fi, etc.

There are four stem-winders included in the monograph: the Audemars-Piguet, Grande Complique—illustrated in the first chapter; the Ekegren "Hindenburg" watch—illustrated in the last chapter; the Swiss "beetle" ring-watch—frontispiece; and, finally, the exceptionally early (circa 1830) Breguet keyless ring-watch—illustrated in Chapter VII, "My Lady's Chamber."

---

* In Figure 24 is a color plate of watch keys.

FIGURE 19

CHAPTER XII

Tsars to Commie-Tsars

In 1844, Tsar Nicholas I of Russia visited Lord Aberdeen in London. The Tsar proposed that—in case of collapse of the Ottoman Empire—Russia and England should consult as to what should be done. Perhaps the first "Gentlemen's Agreement."

This Swiss ruby-cylinder escapement watch (Figure 19 opposite) circa mid-19th century is fitted into a Romanoff silver ruble dated 1844. The making of this very thin movement and the fitting of it into the coin is a mechanical achievement of considerable merit.

In 1844, Russia was only nine years away from the Crimean War during which the "Gentlemen's Agreement" seems to have been abrogated since Britain and France and Florence Nightingale went to the Crimea to save "the sick man of Europe (Turkey)" from Romanoff despotism.

Opposite are four rubles: upper-left commemorates the centennary of the birth of V. I. Lenin (1870-1970); bottom-right commemorates the 20th anniversary of (XXΛET) "Victory over Fascist Germany" (1945-1965).

The other two rubles form the outer case of the watchworks and dial and are actually two rubles cut in half and fitted together.

FIGURE 20

CHAPTER XIII

Hands Up

This late 18th century French watch in a plain gold case is called "in the trade" a "bras-en-l'air." (Figure 20, opposite)

The reason for this is that the owner tells the time by depressing the pendant—that part of the stem of the watch which is below the chain ring. At this point, both arms of the center figure rise to indicate the proper time—hours by the left index finger, minutes by the right index finger.

The mechanical figure on the dial possesses a further intricacy; its head rotates back and forth as though shaking its head at the passage of time. Many of these "bras-en-l'air" do not possess a moveable head.

FIGURE 21

CHAPTER XIV

"C" Stories

It is, perhaps, an interesting historical coincidence that the inventor of the first accurate marine chronometer—John Harrison—died in 1776. His demise was commemorated in England during the same year as the 200th anniversary of United States' independence from that noble land of the Magna Carta.

Charles II of England established the Greenwich Observatory for the main purpose of "rectifying the tables of the motions of the heavens, and the places of the fixed stars, so as to find out the so-much desired LONGITUDE of places for perfecting the art of navigation." The Board of Longitude—created by the British Parliament in the 18th century—offered a twenty thousand pound prize for the completion of a marine timekeeper which would permit the accurate location of a given landfall within 30 minutes of longitude. (In other words, after a six weeks voyage, the timekeeper had to keep *time* within 2 minutes over the whole voyage—that is to say, within three seconds a day. A minute of time represents a linear distance at the equator of nearly 20 miles.)

The test voyage was from the British Isles to Jamaica commencing 18 November 1761 in the good ship *Deptford*. Being of advanced age,

John Harrison requested that his son, William, accompany the "No. 4" marine chronometer on the voyage. So accurately did "No. 4" perform that the *Deptford* reached the Jamaica landfall within 1¼ minutes of longitude—a mere 25 miles away and clearly visible from the "crow's nest." In spite of this accuracy, the Board of Longitude did all in its power to block Harrison from receiving the balance (roughly £10,000) of his prize. It took King George III and a special act of Parliament, finally, to award John Harrison his just due.

The two marine chronometers displayed on page 44 are of about 1820 vintage—one French, one English. Breguet No. 284 has an Earnshaw spring detent escapement and a two-armed compensation balance with helical spring. The brass gimbals are typically Breguet oval-shaped. The English chronometer is by Charles Frodsham, 84 Strand, London, No. 3275, and possesses the more typical circular gimbals.

"Gimbals" is the device which permits the marine chronometer to remain horizontal no matter what the motion of the ship. Sea voyages that you have experienced attest to a maritime motion which suggests a future benefit of "gimbals" being adapted to the human frame!

Belles and Watches

The method of telling time at sea has always been intriguing, and for most mortals totally incomprehensible.

For this reason, there appears opposite a schematic diagram of 24 hours' duration commencing at 8:00 A.M. on any day one chooses. Military time is always represented by four digits: from 0000—midnight, through 2359—one minute before midnight the following day. At sea, this period is divided into six "watches," each of four hours duration: Mid-Watch (0000-0400); Morning Watch (0400-0800); Forenoon Watch (0800-1200); Afternoon Watch (1200-1600); Dog Watch (1600-2000); and finally, First Watch (2000-2400).

Ships Bells and Watches . . .
or the reason for the "Dog Watch"

WATCH	FORENOON		AFTERNOON		DOG		FIRST		MID		MORNING	
	TIME	BELLS	TIME	BELLS	TIME	BELLS	TIME	BELLS	TIME	BELLS	TIME	BELLS
HOURS	0800	8										
	0830	1	1230	1	1630	1	2030	1	2430	1	0430	1
	0900	2	1300	2	1700	2	2100	2	0100	2	0500	2
	0930	3	1330	3	1730	3	2130	3	0130	3	0530	3
	1000	4	1400	4	1800	4	2200	4	0200	4	0600	4
	1030	5	1430	5	1830	1	2230	5	0230	5	0630	5
	1100	6	1500	6	1900	2	2300	6	0300	6	0700	6
	1130	7	1530	7	1930	3	2330	7	0330	7	0730	7
	1200	8	1600	8	2000	8	2400	8	0400	8	0800	8

The probable reason for this extraordinary "time" scheme is constant motion! Except in drydock, a boat or a ship is in constant motion and its crew—or part of it—must be constantly vigilant. Hence, the crew is divided into "watches" and experience has shown that four hours is about as long as the average human being can remain alert without a change of venue.

Also (1) the crew must eat at least one hot, copious meal, and (2) rotation of watches must be provided for, so that one faction of the crew does not constantly have the same time on duty, for instance, the Mid-Watch, from midnight to 0400. Both of these aims are accomplished by dividing the Dog Watch * (1600-2000) into two equal parts. Thus the crew can be fed in two shifts and also this provides, for instance, that the Afternoon Watch on Monday rotates to have the Mid-Watch on Tuesday, etc.

Returning to ship's bells, the collection contains a ship's bell clock made by Charles Frodsham of London in the early 1950's which, indeed, does strike the Dog Watch, namely 4 bells at 1800; 1 bell at 1830; 2 bells at 1900; 3 bells at 1930; and then back to 8 bells at 2000. During no other Watch does this irregularity take place.

The clock *case* of this Frodsham clock is an identical copy of the clock *case* of the Breguet "sympathique" clock currently in the possession of Queen Elizabeth II in Buckingham Palace.

* See footnote following page.

"Footnote"

THE UNIVERSITY OF ALABAMA
COLLEGE OF ARTS AND SCIENCES
UNIVERSITY, ALABAMA 35486

DEPARTMENT OF PHILOSOPHY
P. O. BOX 6289

September 26
1976

Dear Peter:

Herewith a preliminary report on the phrase 'dog watch'—at least I hope it is preliminary because the results so far are not very satisfactory. I have consulted various dictionaries and encyclopedias, and my linguist friends—the word boys—have consulted other far more specialized works. But the more we consult, the worse the confusion becomes confounded. For the simple truth appears to be that nobody knows where the phrase originated, or why dog watches are called such.

Regarding the date at which the phrase came into use there is general agreement: it appeared during the latter part of the 17th century, and the earliest recorded appearance in print is 1708.

But the derivation is another matter. There seems to be four principal explanations:

1. It is a corruption of 'dodged' watch: on the basis that you dodge, or miss, half the time of the usual watch.
2. It is a corruption of 'docked' watch: a watch from which something is taken away, as in docked pay.
3. It derives from the phrase 'dog sleep,' which in turn means an interrupted sleep: hence an interrupted watch.
4. It is a watch that is "cur-tailed"!

I talked today with another friend who is an expert on naval history, and he does not know the derivation but rather suspects that it may derive from some Dutch word or phrase, as British sailors were then much under Dutch influence. There was a common Dutch type of ship called "dogger," but he knows of no connection between this and the watch.

Personally, I prefer number 4 above. But it has the least support among the word boys. Opinion is about evenly divided among the other three.

My chief word boy here is going to write to a friend of his on the West coast who is an even bigger word boy and see if he can contribute anything. So I'll hope to be in touch again.

In the meantime, thanks again so much for the lovely weekend. Lawson joins me in love to Mary and yourself. Hope Mary enjoyed the Paris opera. I am afraid that she sacrificed her La Scala tickets for our enjoyment.

As ever, Ginx (Jenkins)

P.S.—Don't think for a moment that you are causing a lot of work and trouble here. Quite to the contrary. There is nothing a scholar—especially a retired one like my local word boy—loves more than an unsolved problem. All of this will probably lead to at least three articles!   G.

FIGURE 22

CHAPTER XV

Fuehrer's Feuer

With the hydrogen explosion of the airship *Hindenburg* at 7:25 p.m. on Ascension Day—6 May 1937—the Hitlerian juggernaut received its first irretrievable reverse which would culminate in the Bunkers of Berlin eight years later.

To those who believe in sabotage, or to those who believe in the static electricity theory of destruction—either way—the holocaust was so graphically chronicled that there can be little argument about many of the happenings during those lurid 90 seconds between the moment of the initial explosion and the time that the aluminum skeleton lay stark on the airfield. In any event, international commercial lighter-than-air flights came to an end that evening at Lakehurst, New Jersey.

The collection contains a fob-watch worn by the author at the time of the crash (Figure 22). A detail of this watch appears on the following page, and it is interesting to note that the inscription reads, in part, "Recovered intact near the wreckage—Lakehurst, May 7, 1937." This latter date is occasioned by the fact that, while the watch fell out of the owner's waistcoat pocket onto the sand of the airfield on the evening of 6 May, the watch was indeed, recovered by officials of the Deutsche Zeppelin Rederei assisted by the U.S. Navy and representatives of the U.S. Department of Commerce on 7 May. In addition, while the inscription states that the watch was "worn by Peter Belin," the name "Ferdinand Lammot Belin, Jr., February 3, 1934" is inscribed in the middle of the inside back of the watch (Figure 23). These names represent one and the same person who changed his name legally shortly after he attained the age of 21 years. The watch itself is a 21st birthday present to the author from his uncle, Pierre S. DuPont.

The watch was purchased from J. E. Caldwell & Co. in Philadelphia but is of Swiss origin by the maker Edouard Koehn who was at that time associated with H. K. Ekegren of Geneva. That the watch is of the finest work is attested to by the fact that it bears the official Geneva "watch seal" in testimony of its "exceptional (thin) design and craftsmanship."

Koehn—a man of outstanding erudition—nevertheless got himself in dire trouble with the U.S. Customs, allegedly for smuggling watches into the United States for sale on the American market. It is said that this ruined Koehn financially and caused him to continue to produce high-grade watches until a very advanced age; he died at 84 years in the early 1960s.

FIGURE 23

FIGURE 24

FIGURE 25

FIGURE 26

FIGURE 27

FIGURE 28

FIGURE 29

FIGURE 30

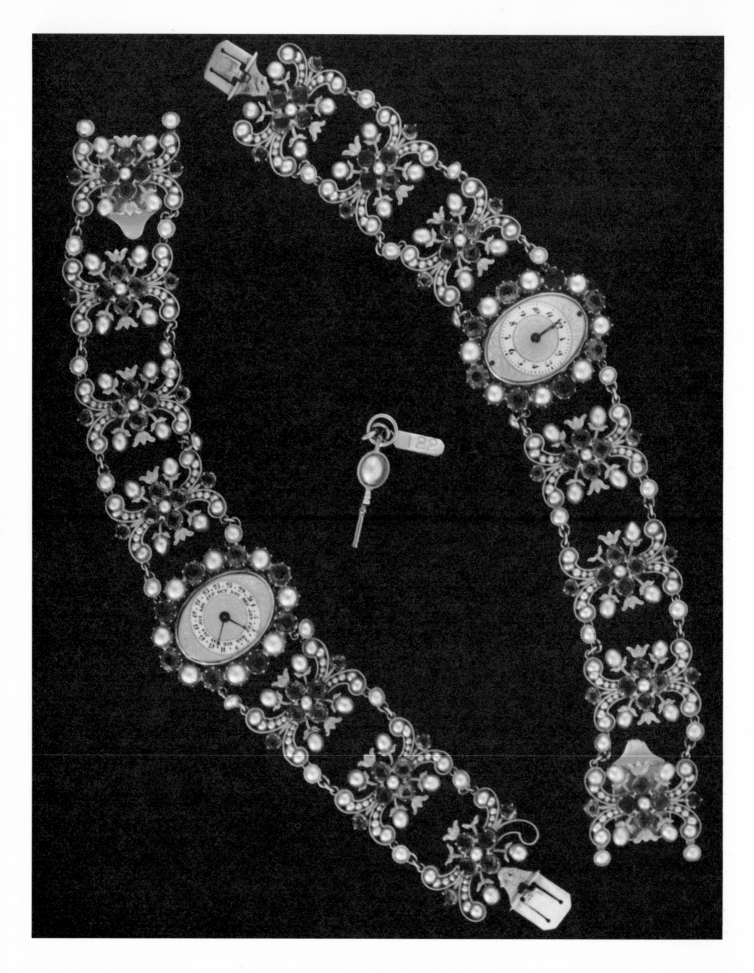

FIGURE 31

EPILOGUE

Time is man made
Difficult of conception
Often overlooked
Never retrieved.